First published in 2019 by Modern Toss Ltd.
Modern Toss, PO Box 386, Brighton BN1 3SN, England
www.moderntoss.com

ISBN 978-0-9929107-8-5

The Desperate Business cartoons first appeared in Private Eye.

Text and illustrations copyright © Modern Toss Limited 2019.
PO Box 386, Brighton BN1 3SN, England.

The right of Jon Link and Mick Bunnage to be identified as the
authors of this work has been asserted by them in accordance
with the Copyright, Designs and Patents Act 1988.

A CIP catalogue record for this book is available from the British Library.

Designed and typeset by Modern Toss.

Visit www.moderntoss.com to read more about all our books and to buy them yeah.
You will also find lots of other shit there, and you can sign up to our mailing list so
that you're always kept bang up to date with it, cheers.

MODERN TOSS PRESENTS

by Jon Link and Mick Bunnage

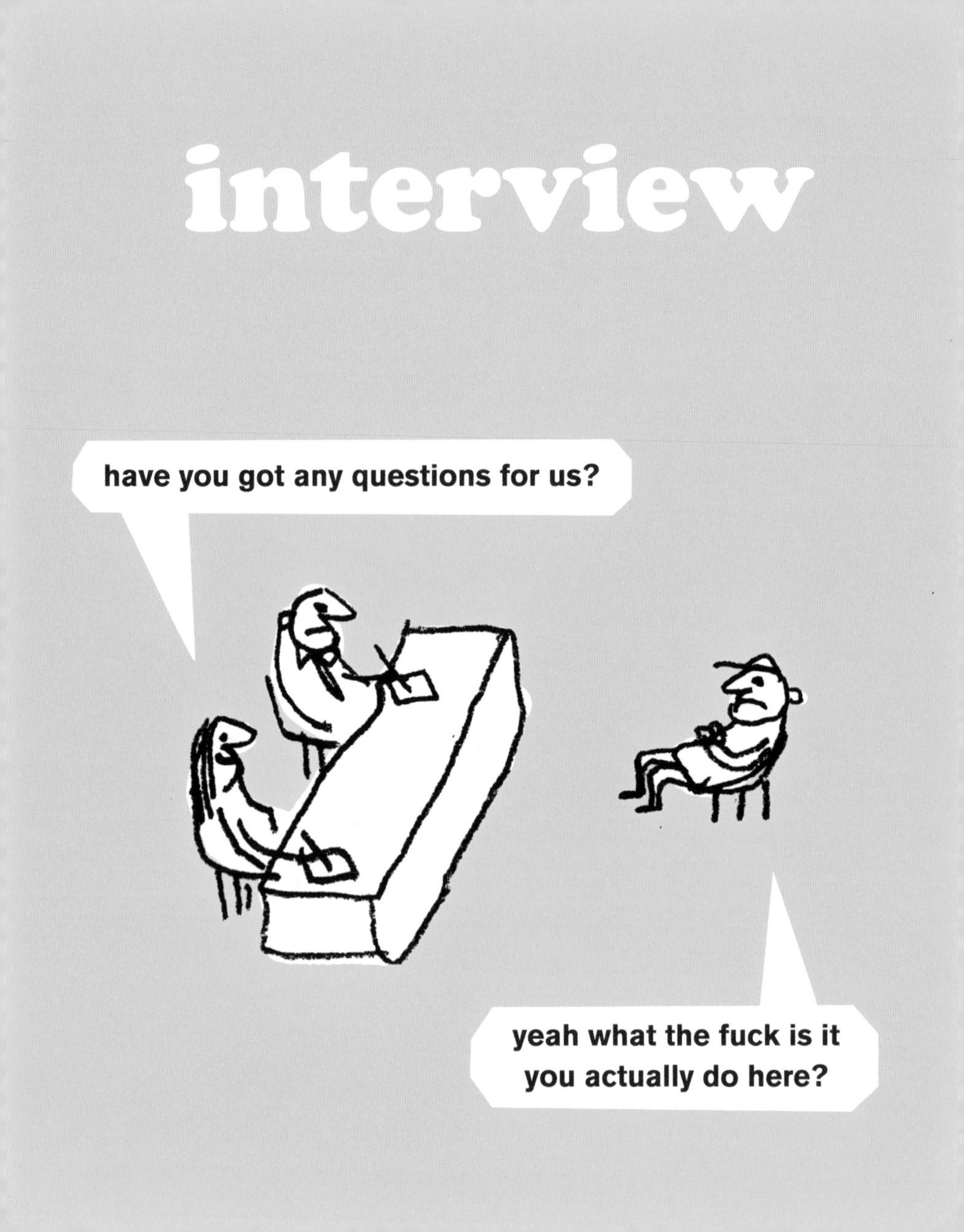
interview
have you got any questions for us?
yeah what the fuck is it
you actually do here?

work

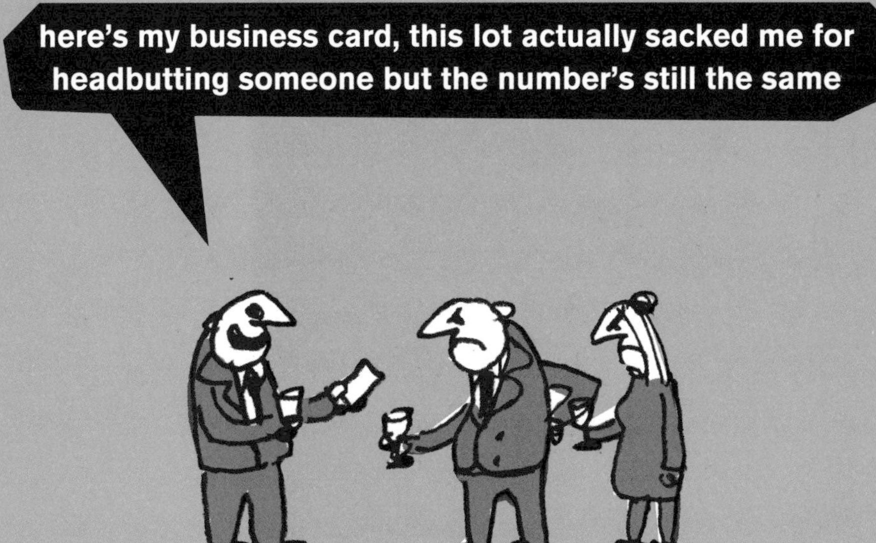
here's my business card, this lot actually sacked me for headbutting someone but the number's still the same

work

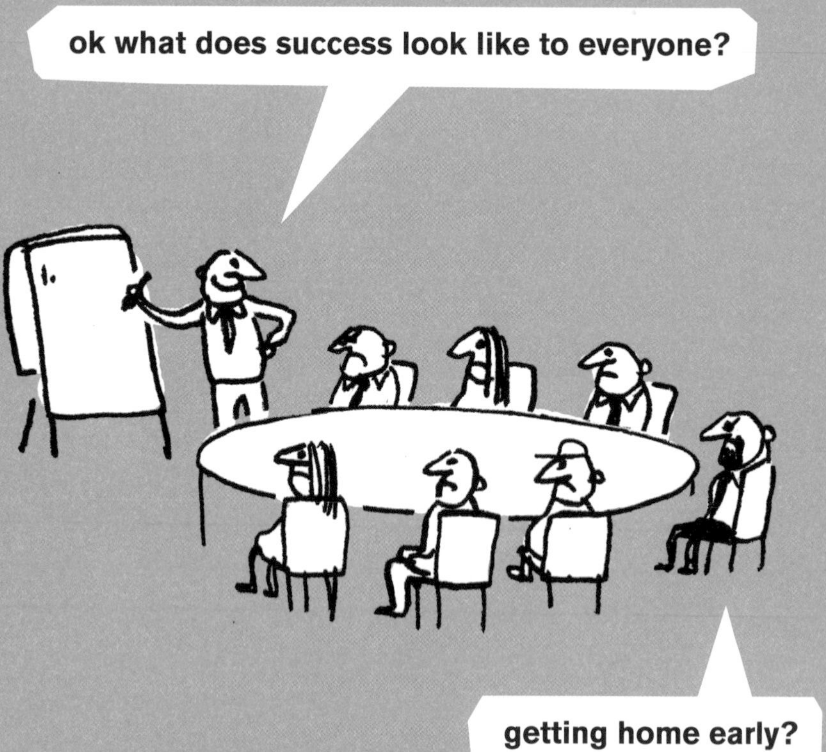
ok what does success look like to everyone?
1.
getting home early?

work

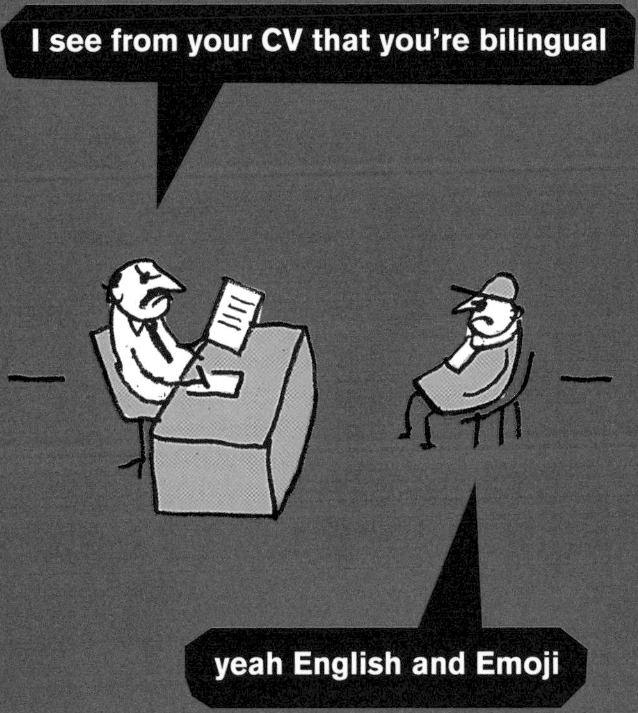
I see from your CV that you're bilingual
yeah English and Emoji

work

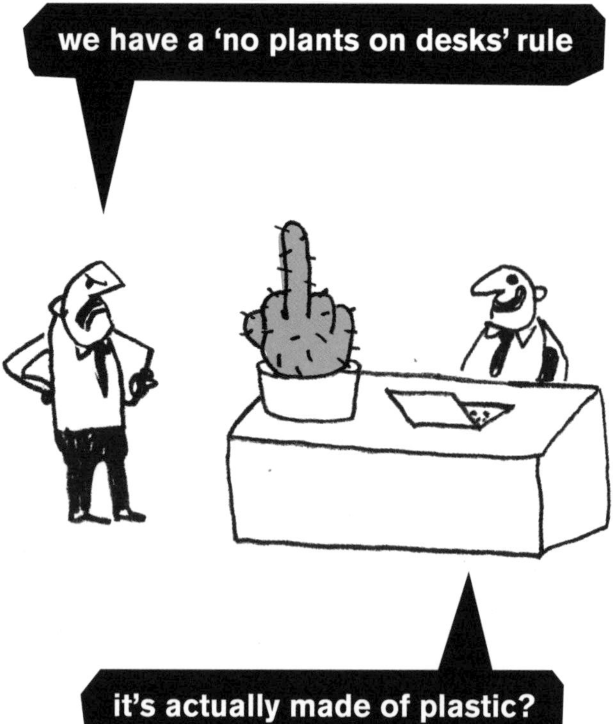
we have a ‘no plants on desks’ rule
it’s actually made of plastic?

work

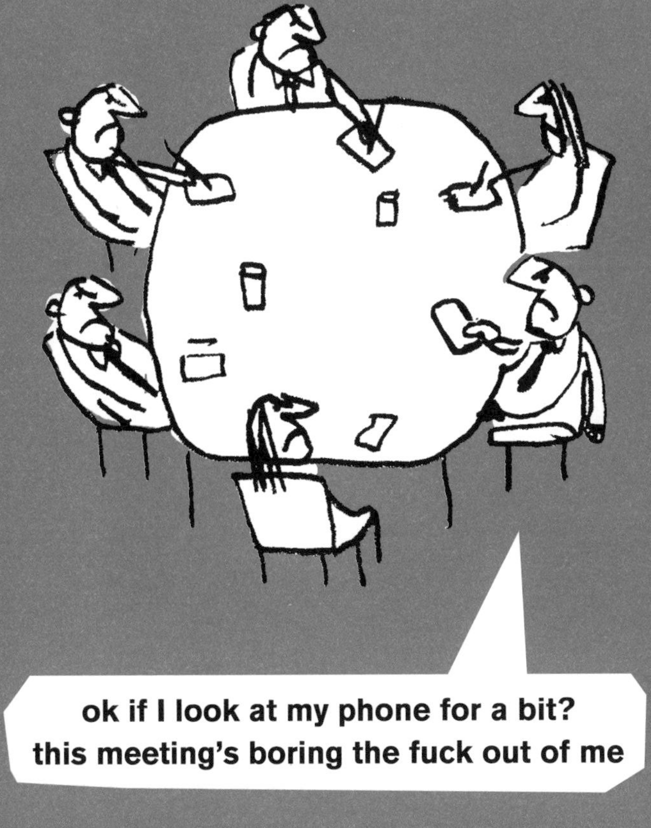
ok if I look at my phone for a bit?
this meeting's boring the fuck out of me

work

he's very strong on disruption techniques

interview

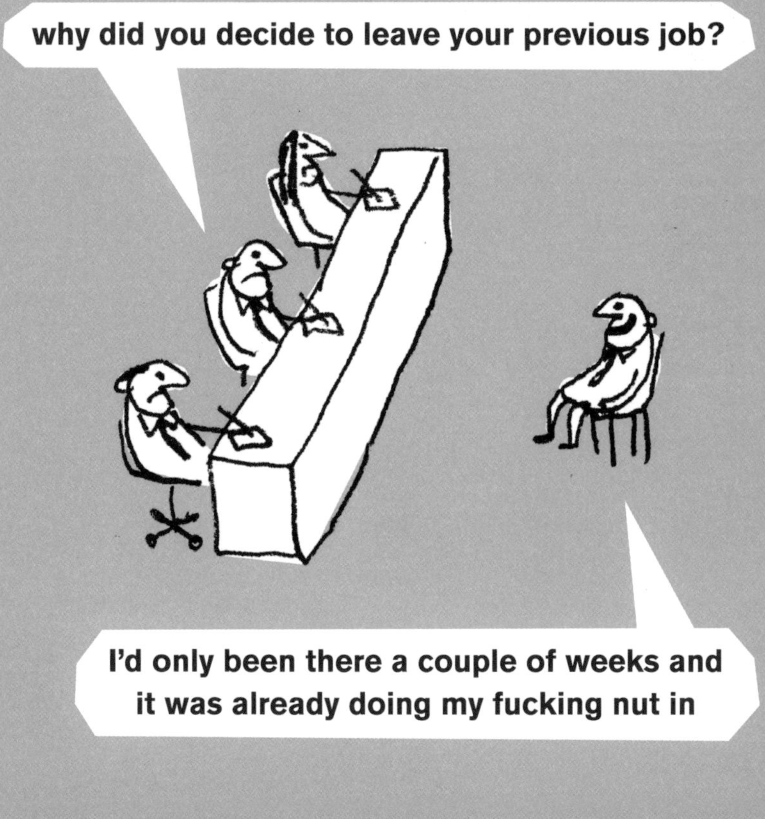
why did you decide to leave your previous job?
I'd only been there a couple of weeks and it was already doing my fucking nut in

work

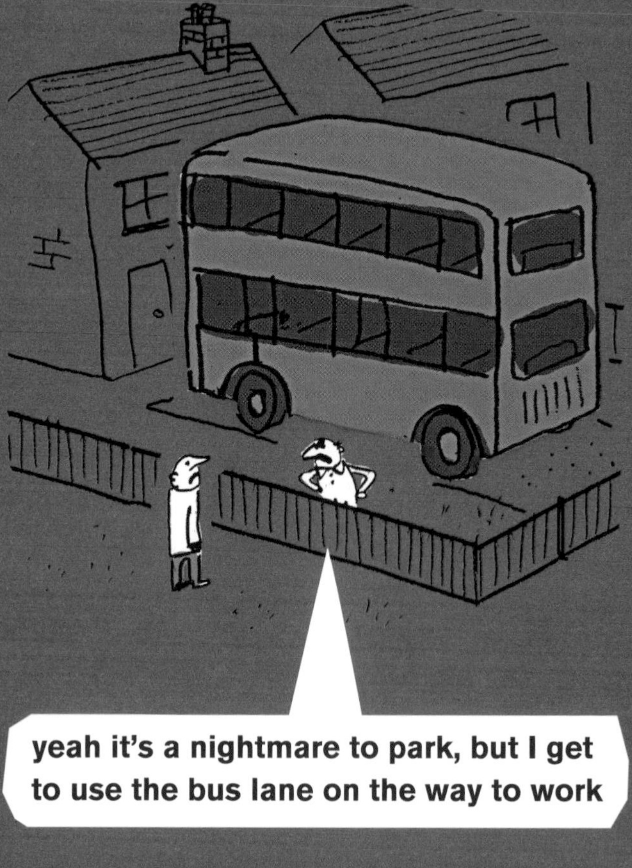
yeah it's a nightmare to park, but I get to use the bus lane on the way to work

work

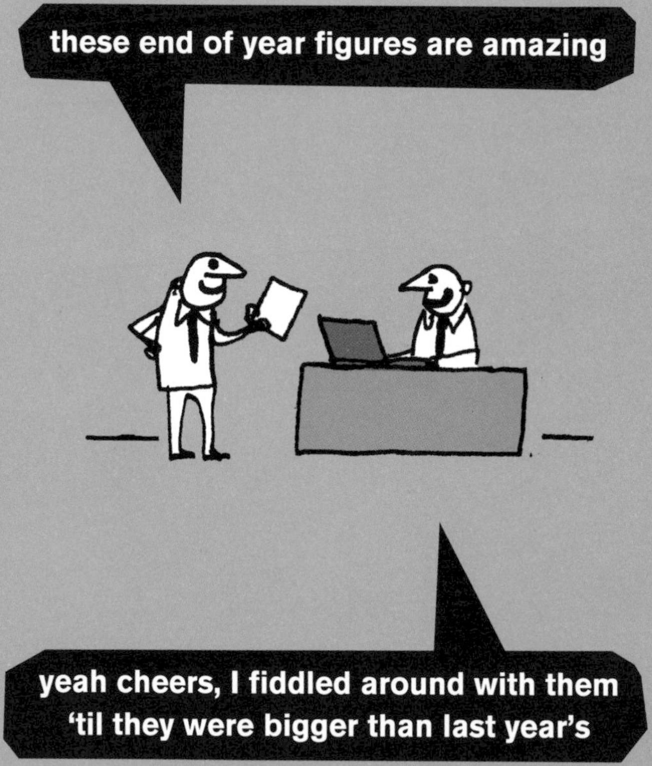
these end of year figures are amazing
yeah cheers, I fiddled around with them 'til they were bigger than last year's

work

what's all these photos of you naked?
just letting you know what I've got if you need to do a company calendar

interview

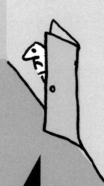

I was just doing a power pose to boost my confidence levels and I've actually gone and shat meself, any chance we could reschedule?

work

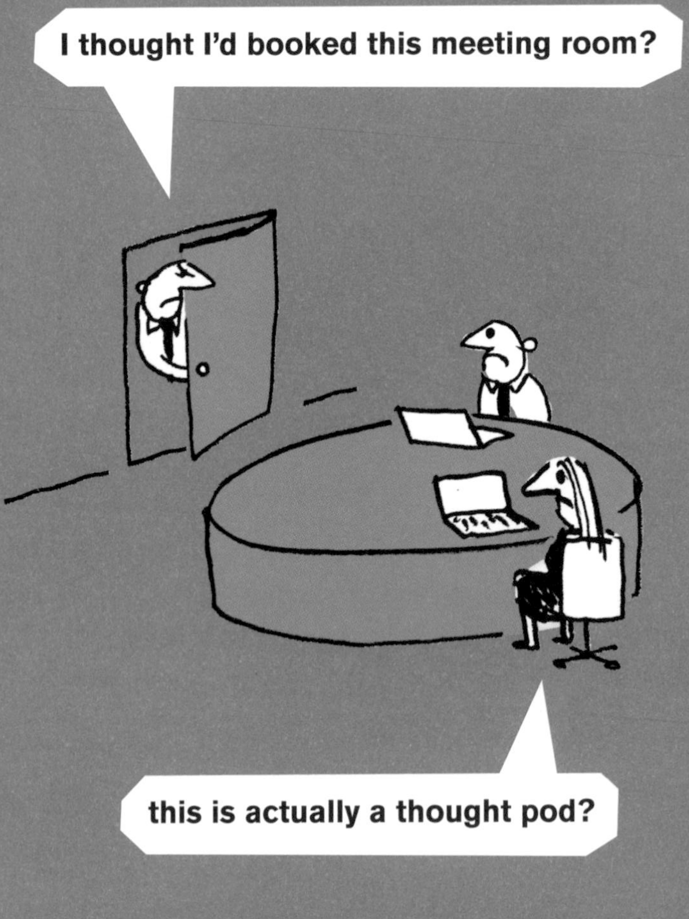
I thought I'd booked this meeting room?
this is actually a thought pod?

work

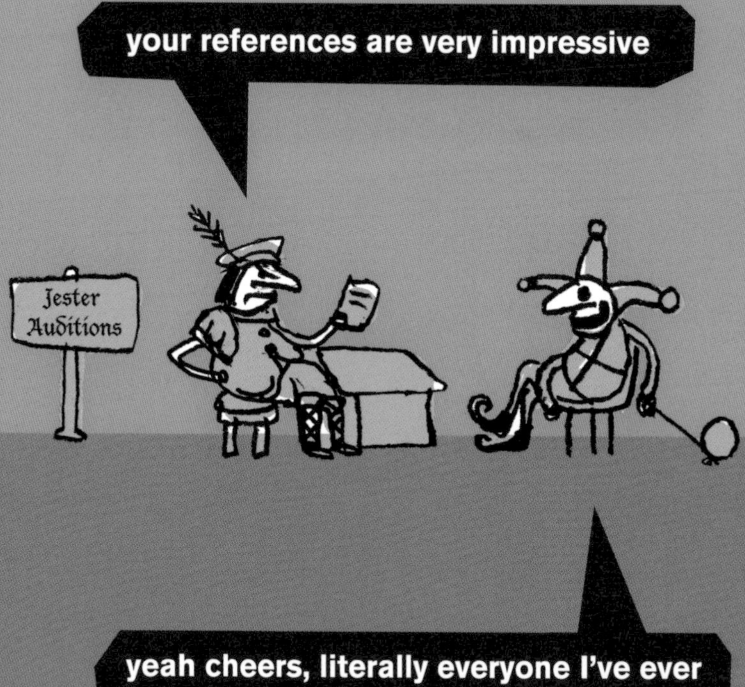
your references are very impressive
Jester Auditions
yeah cheers, literally everyone I've ever met says I'm a total fucking idiot

work

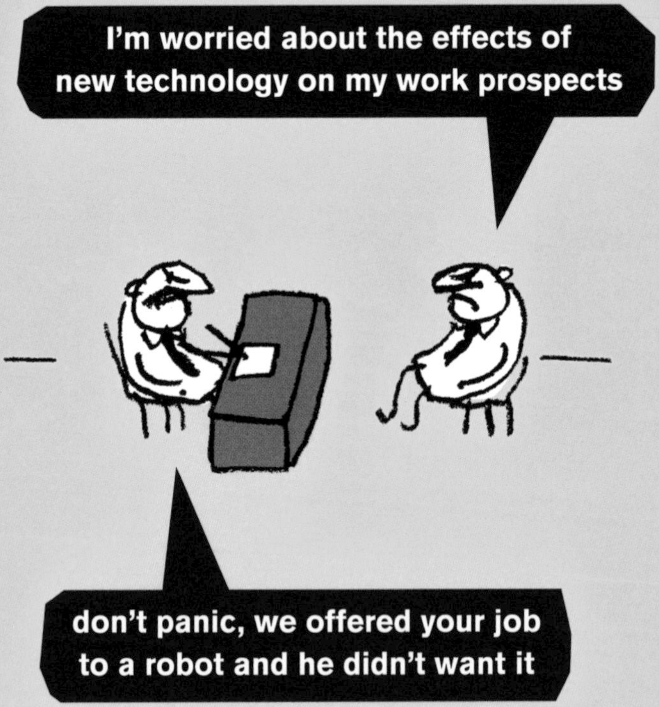
I'm worried about the effects of new technology on my work prospects
don't panic, we offered your job to a robot and he didn't want it

interview

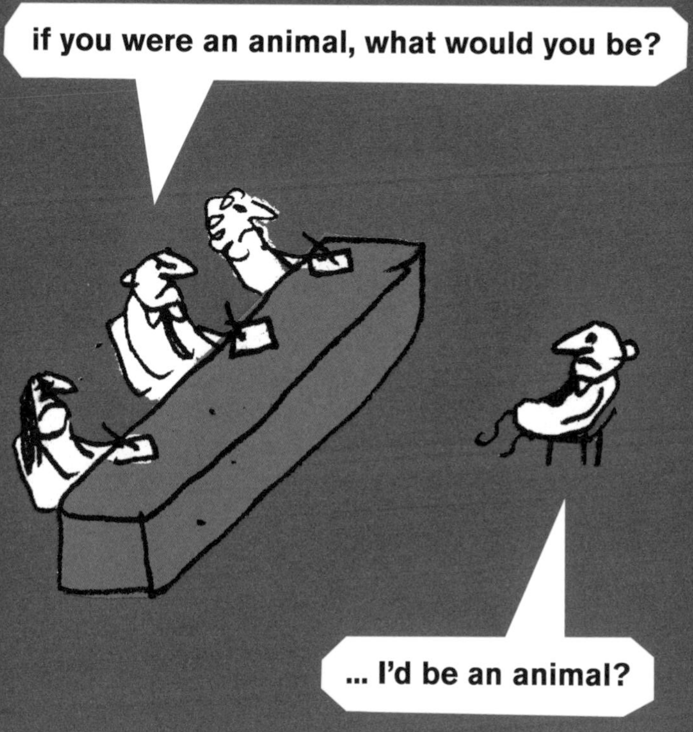
if you were an animal, what would you be?
... I'd be an animal?

work

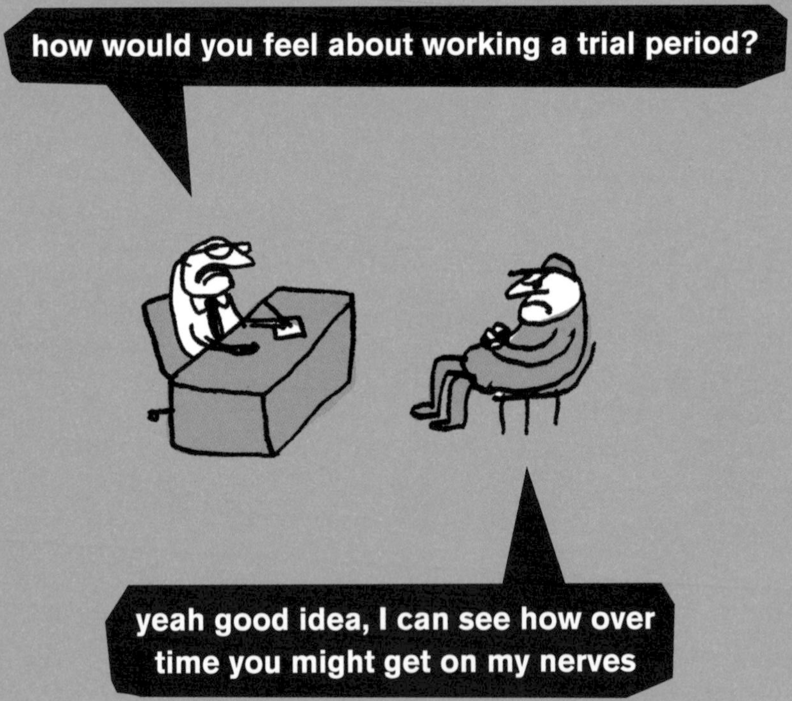
how would you feel about working a trial period?
yeah good idea, I can see how over time you might get on my nerves

work

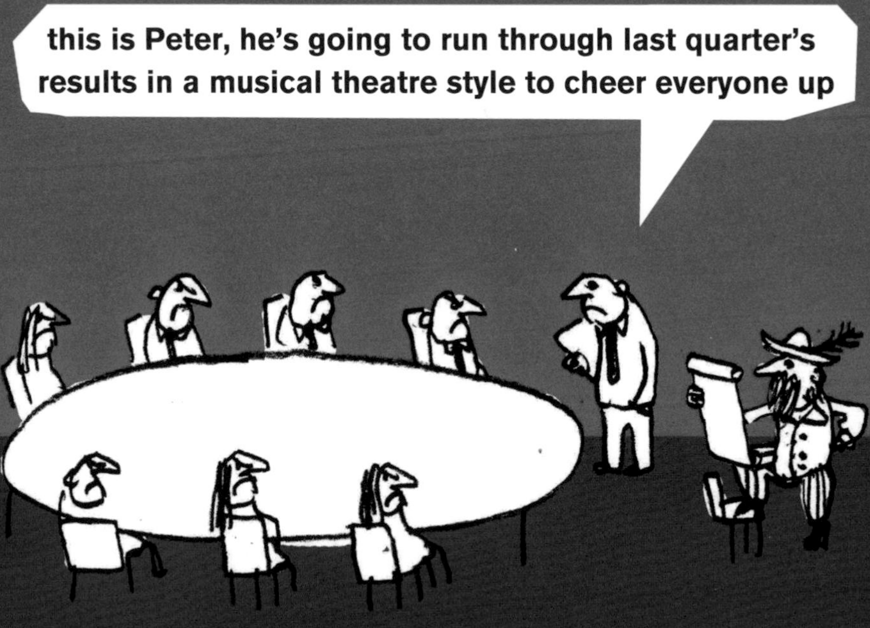
this is Peter, he's going to run through last quarter's results in a musical theatre style to cheer everyone up

work

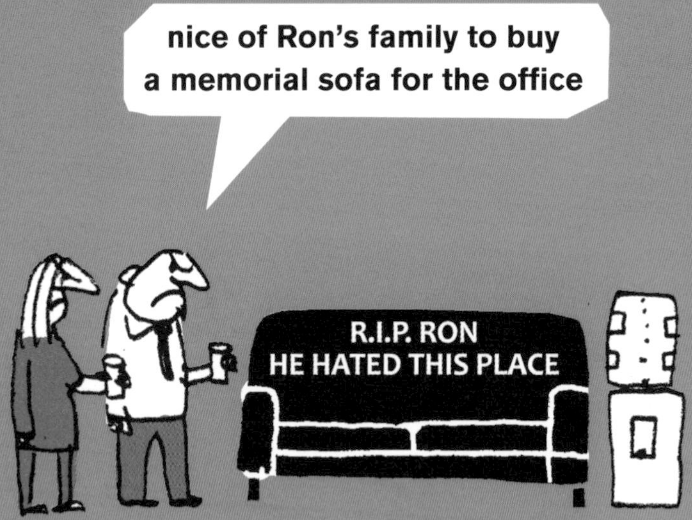
nice of Ron's family to buy a memorial sofa for the office
R.I.P. RON
HE HATED THIS PLACE

work

your references are terrible
if they were any good I wouldn't be sat here trying to get a new job

work

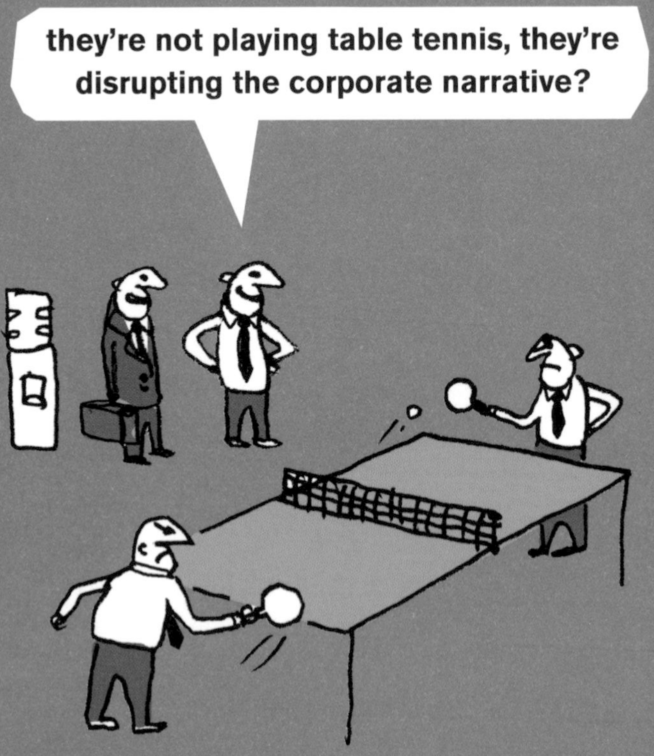
they're not playing table tennis, they're disrupting the corporate narrative?

work

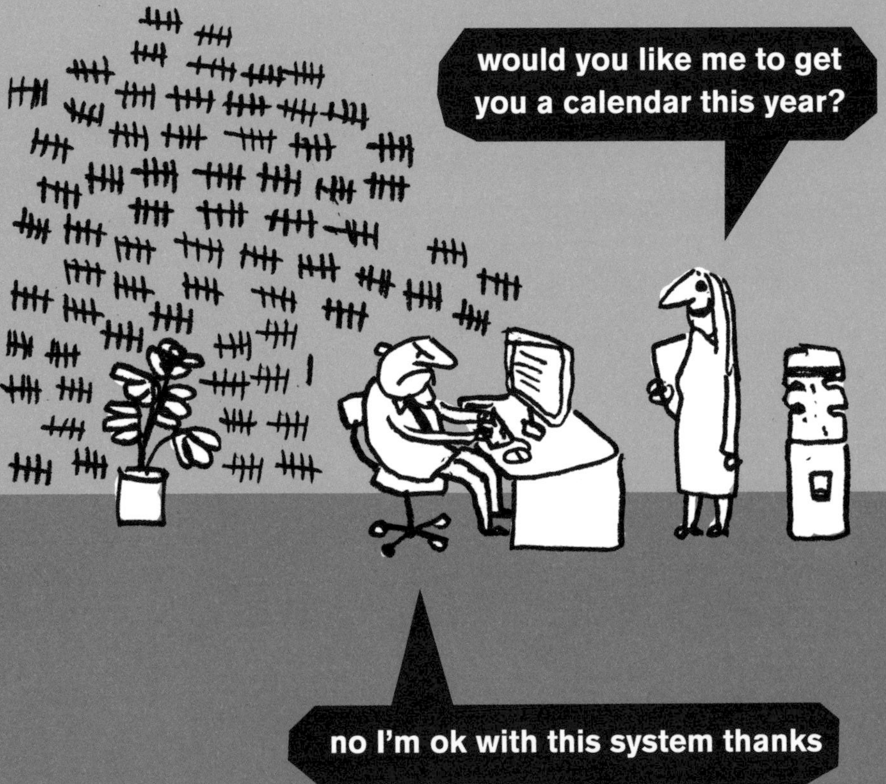
would you like me to get you a calendar this year?
no I'm ok with this system thanks

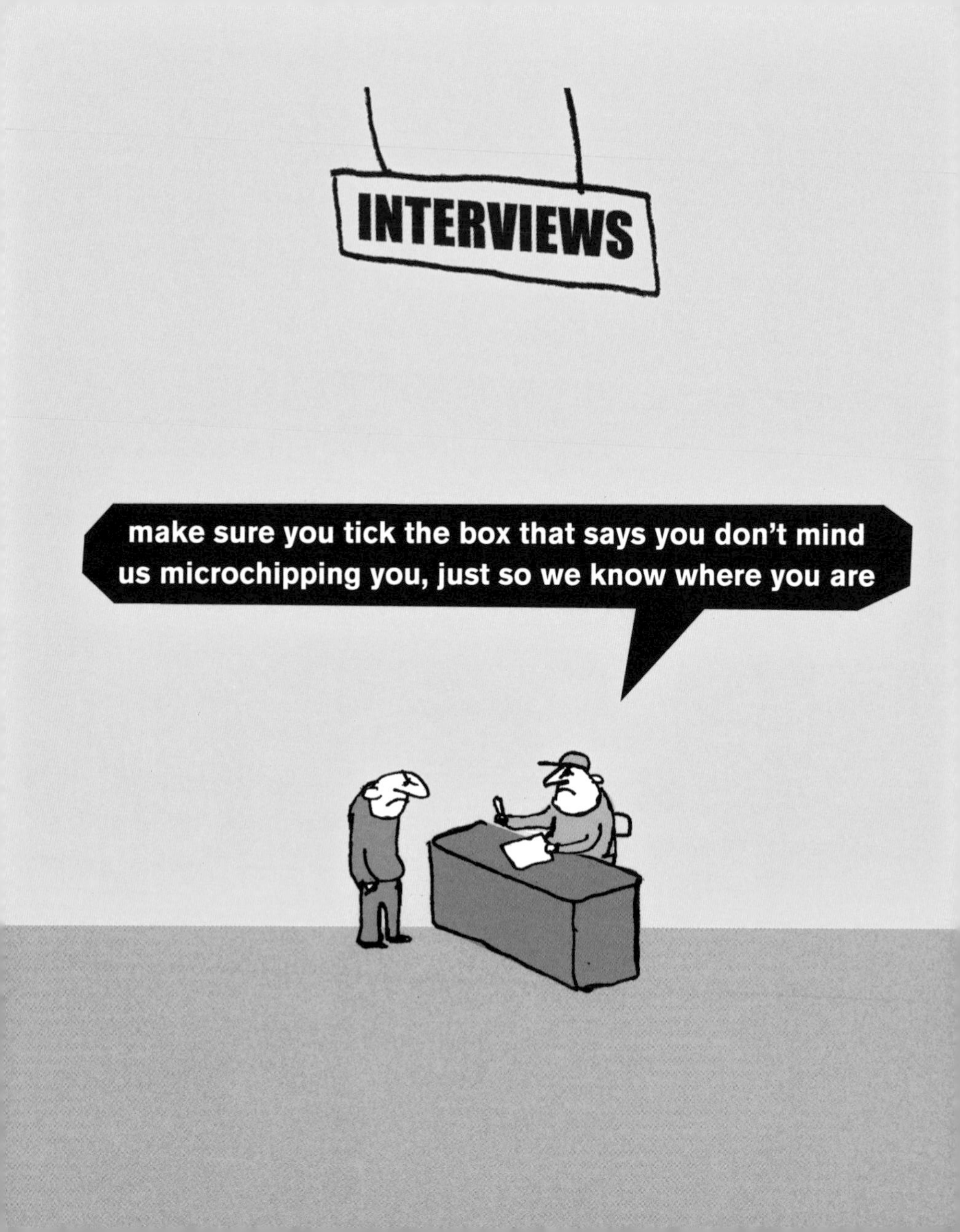
INTERVIEWS
make sure you tick the box that says you don't mind us microchipping you, just so we know where you are

work

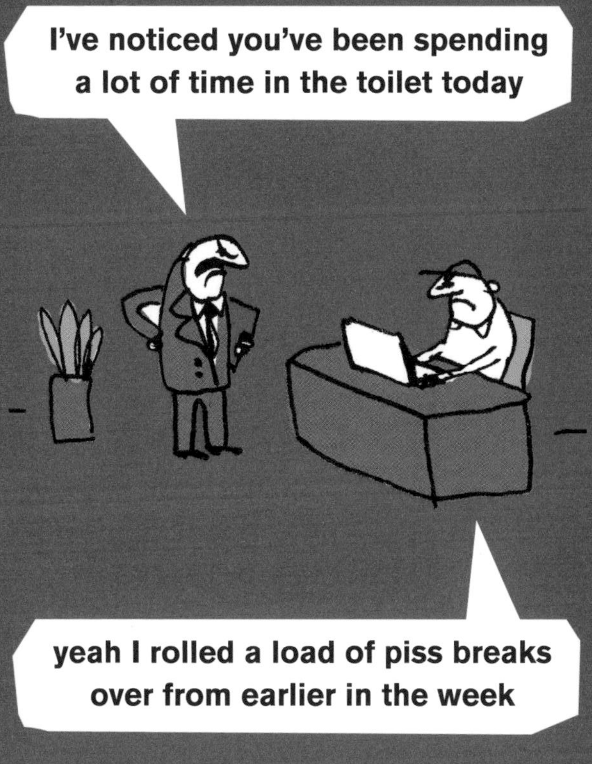
I've noticed you've been spending a lot of time in the toilet today
yeah I rolled a load of piss breaks over from earlier in the week

work

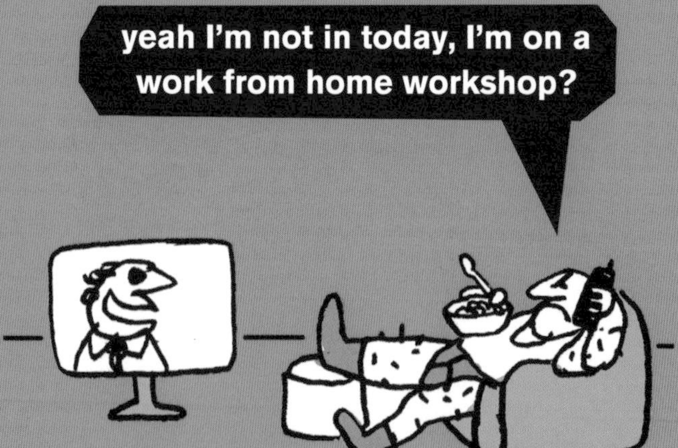
yeah I'm not in today, I'm on a work from home workshop?

work

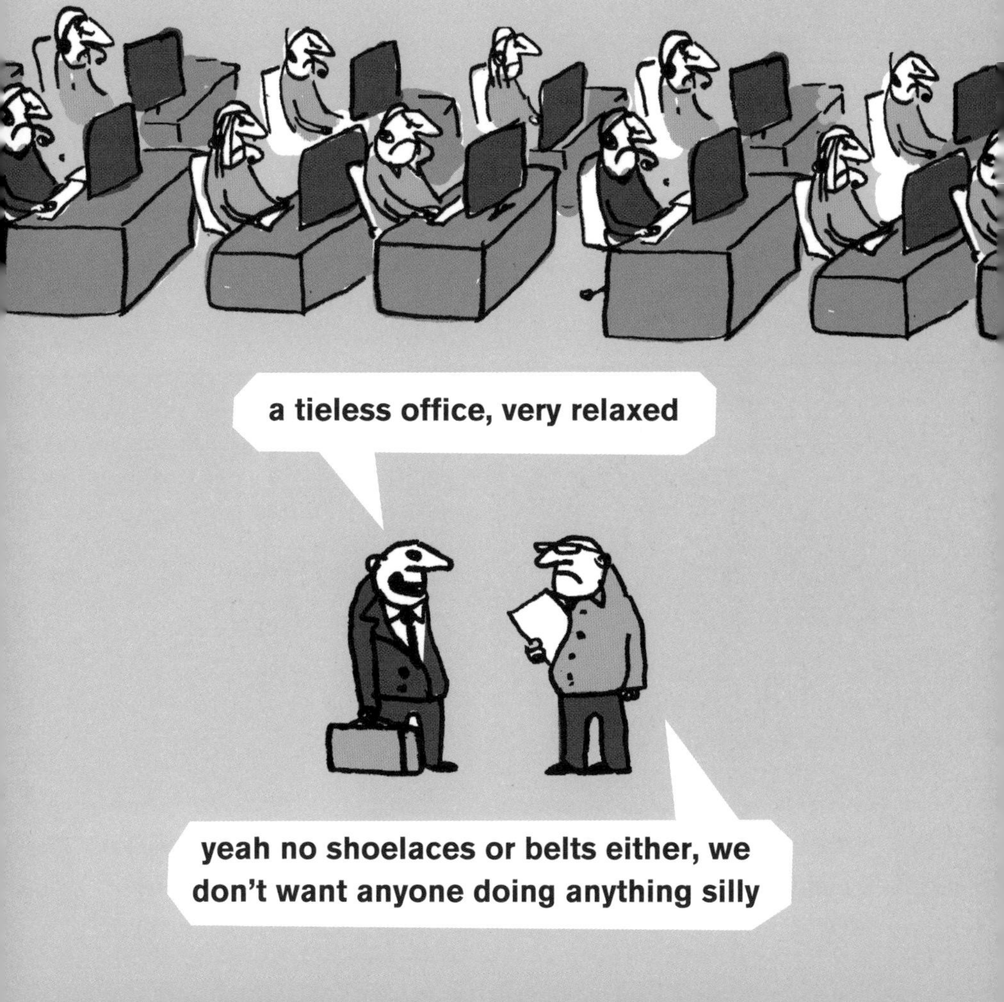
a tieless office, very relaxed
yeah no shoelaces or belts either, we don't want anyone doing anything silly

work

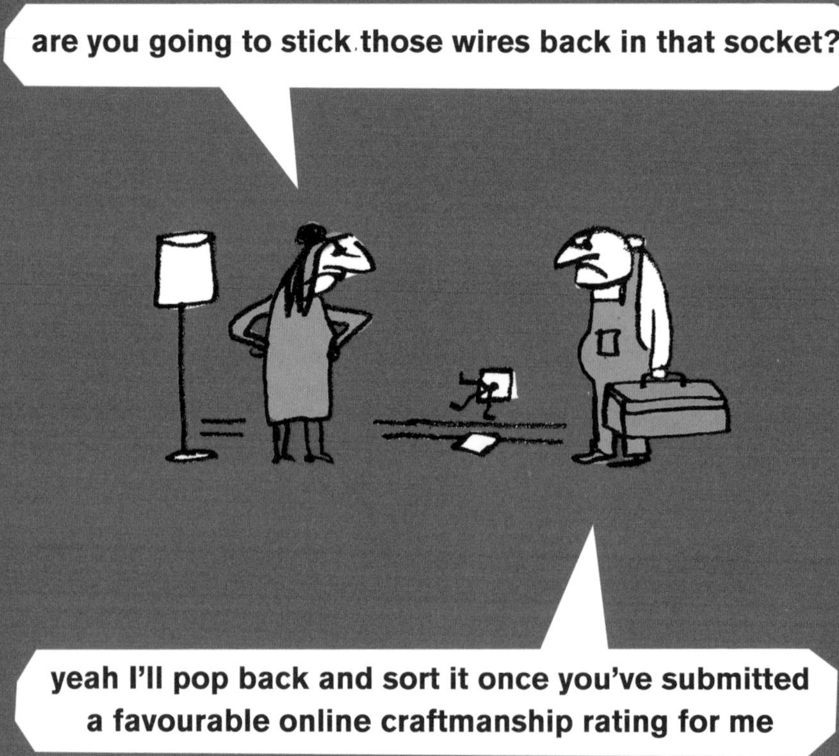
are you going to stick those wires back in that socket?
yeah I'll pop back and sort it once you've submitted a favourable online craftmanship rating for me

work

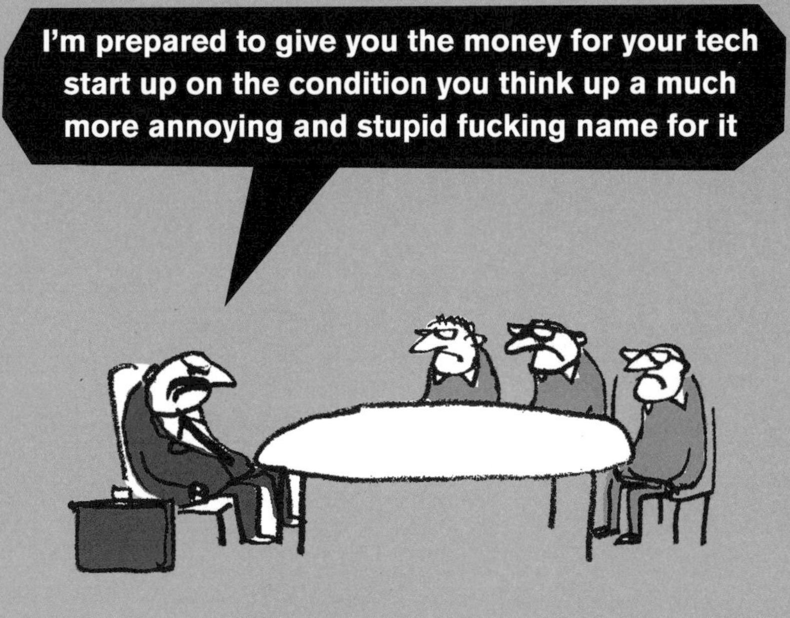
I'm prepared to give you the money for your tech start up on the condition you think up a much more annoying and stupid fucking name for it

work

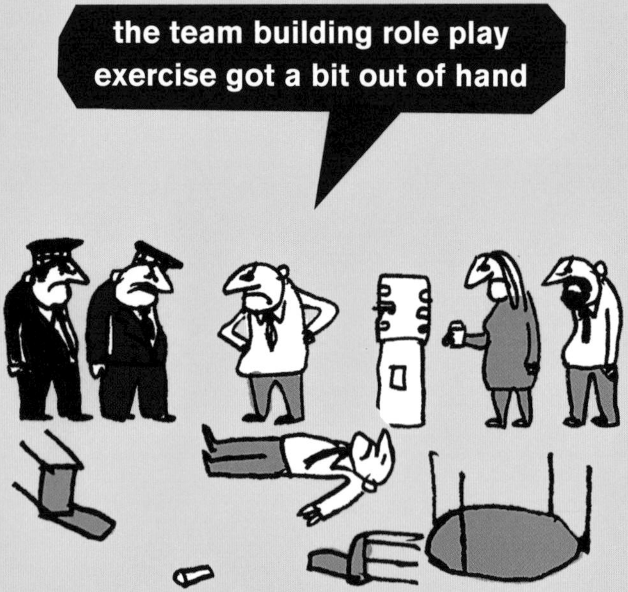
the team building role play exercise got a bit out of hand

work

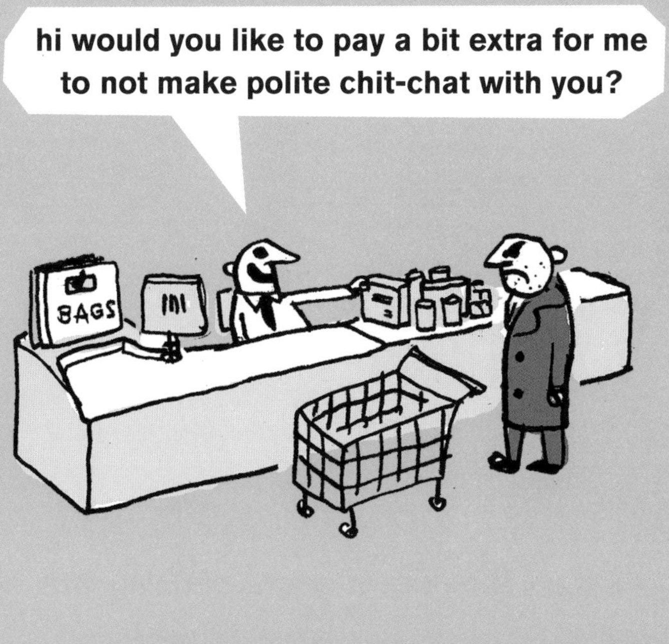
hi would you like to pay a bit extra for me to not make polite chit-chat with you?
BAGS

work

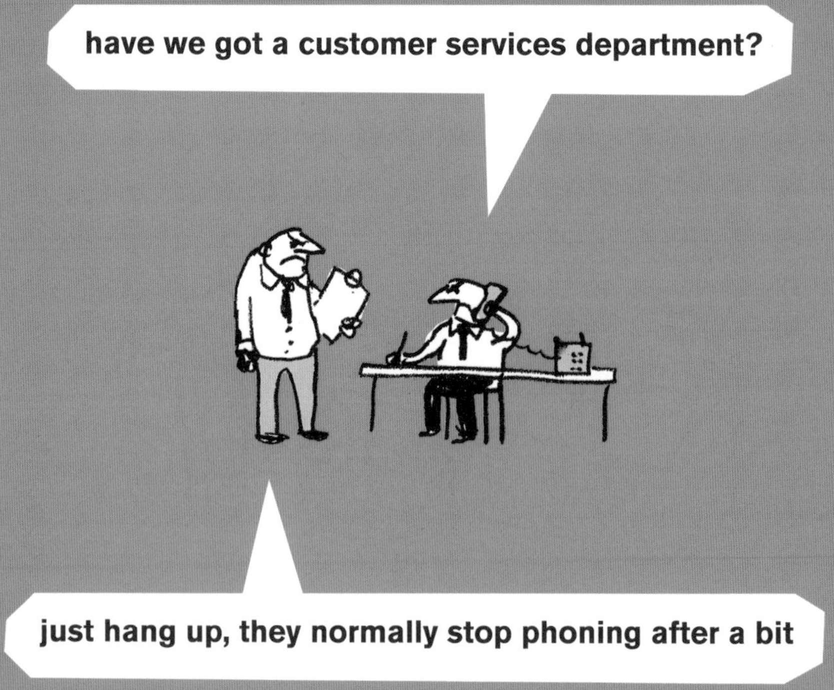
have we got a customer services department?
just hang up, they normally stop phoning after a bit

health & safety

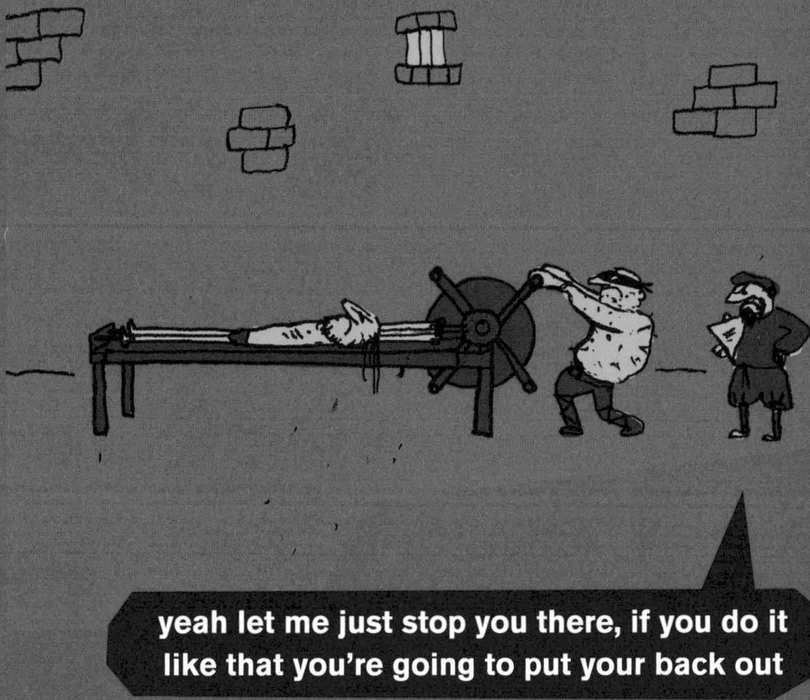
yeah let me just stop you there, if you do it like that you're going to put your back out

interview

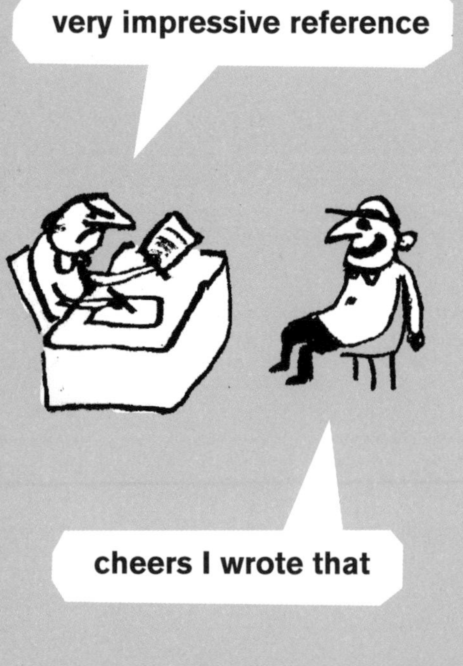
very impressive reference
cheers I wrote that

work

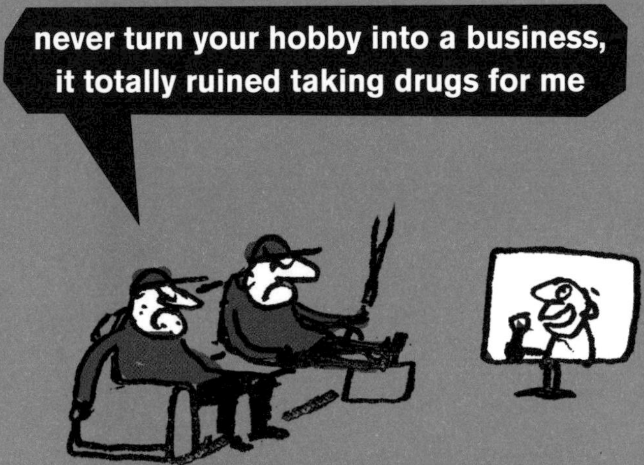
never turn your hobby into a business, it totally ruined taking drugs for me

work

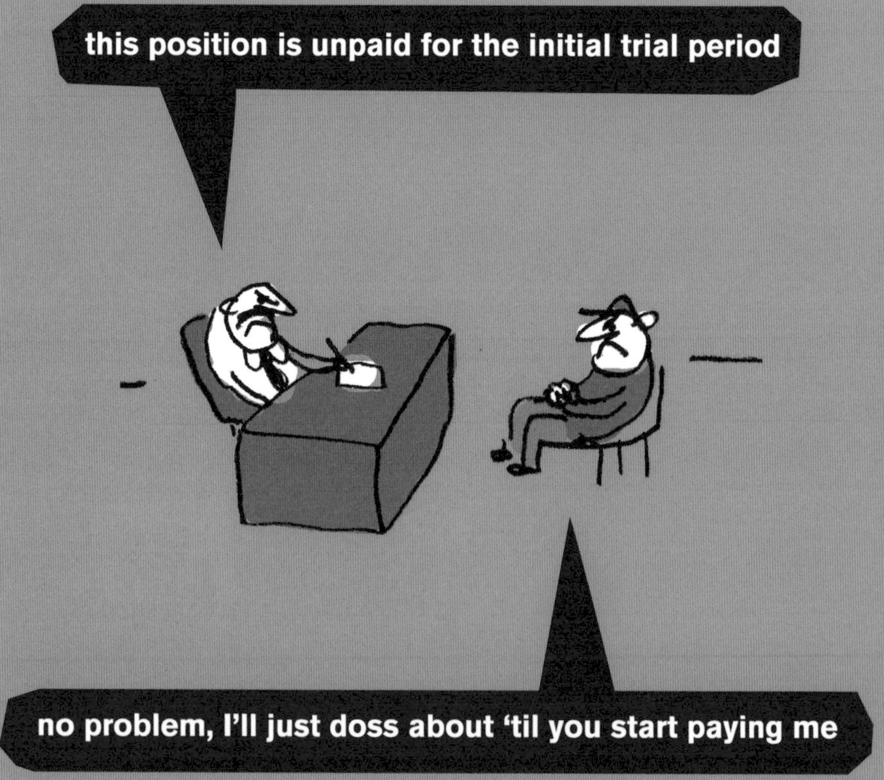
this position is unpaid for the initial trial period
no problem, I'll just doss about 'til you start paying me

work

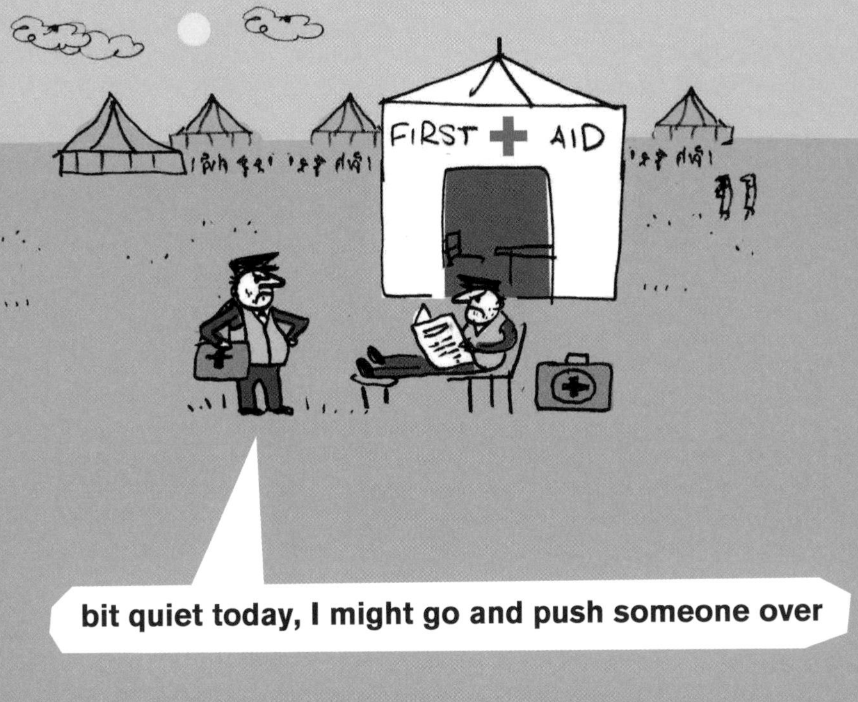
FIRST AID
bit quiet today, I might go and push someone over

work

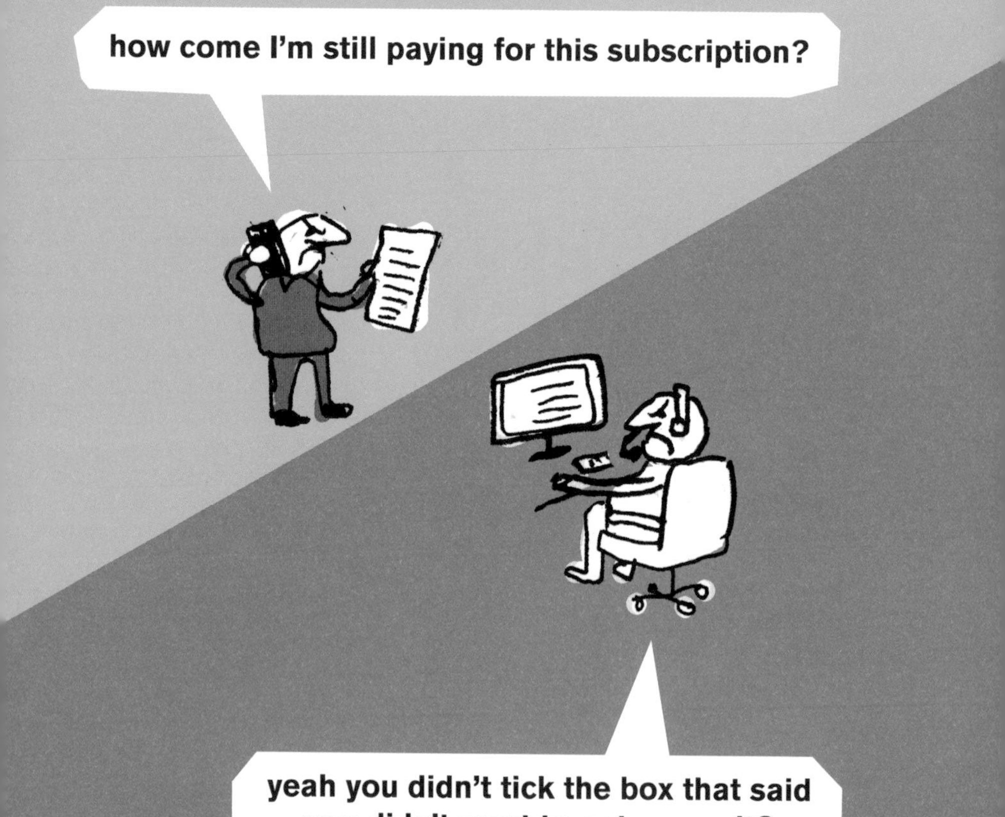
how come I'm still paying for this subscription?
yeah you didn't tick the box that said you didn't want to not renew it?

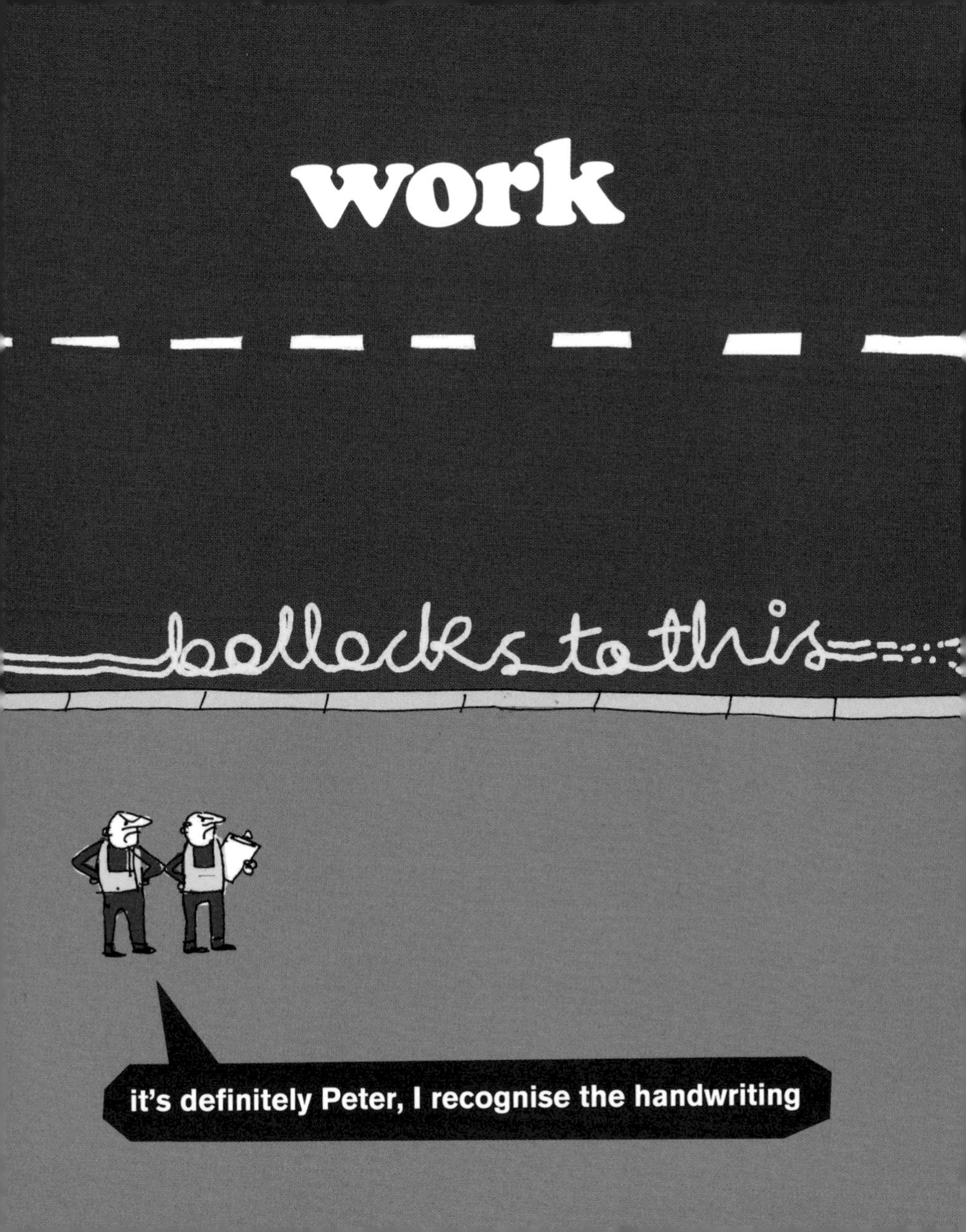
work
bollocks to this
it's definitely Peter, I recognise the handwriting

work

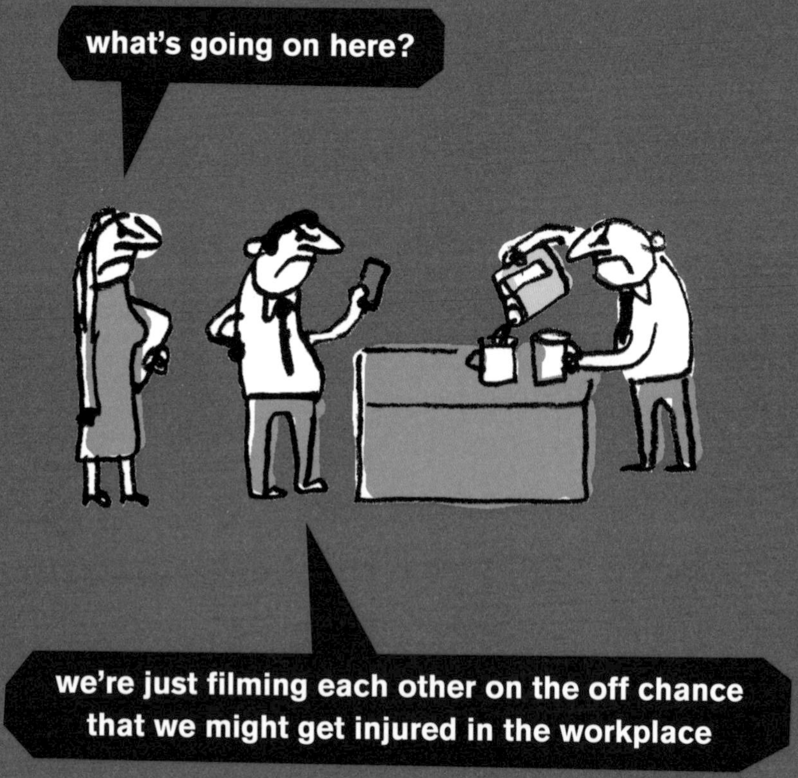
what's going on here?
we're just filming each other on the off chance that we might get injured in the workplace

work

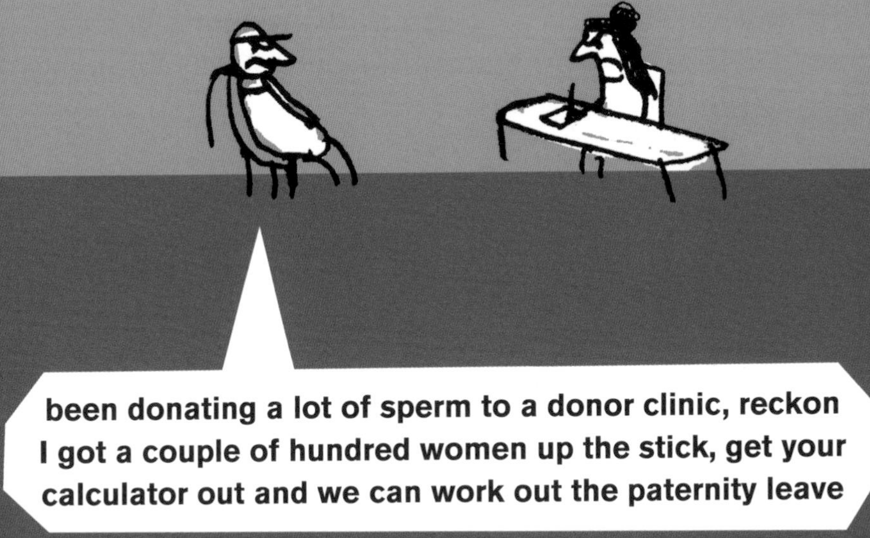

been donating a lot of sperm to a donor clinic, reckon I got a couple of hundred women up the stick, get your calculator out and we can work out the paternity leave

meeting

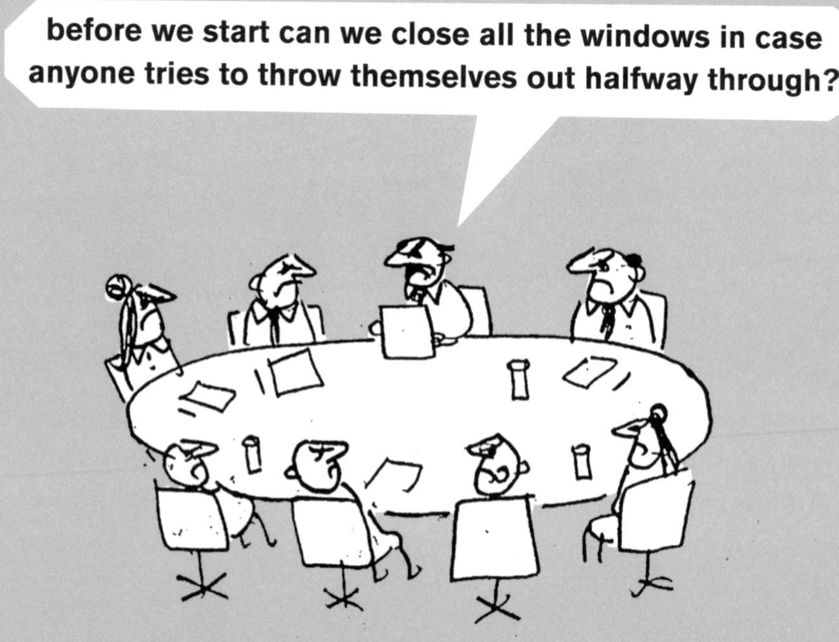
before we start can we close all the windows in case anyone tries to throw themselves out halfway through?

work

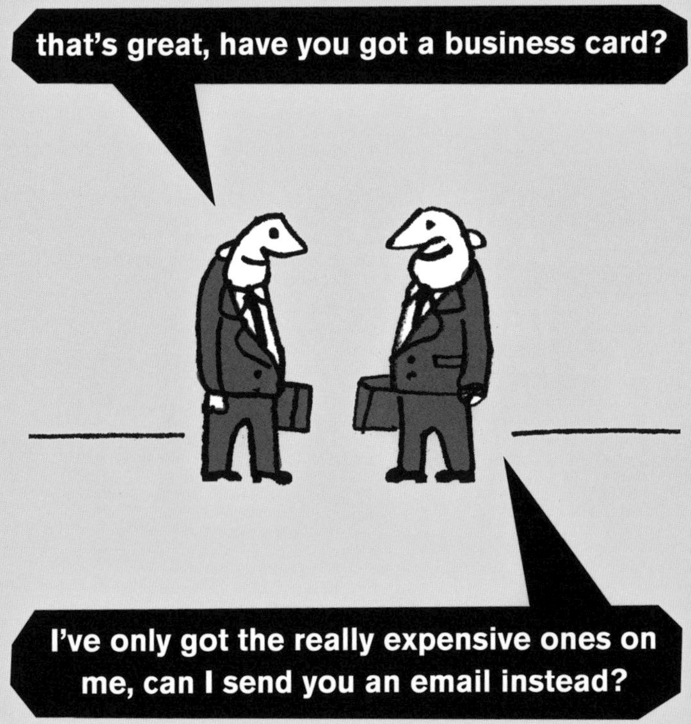
that's great, have you got a business card?
I've only got the really expensive ones on me, can I send you an email instead?

work

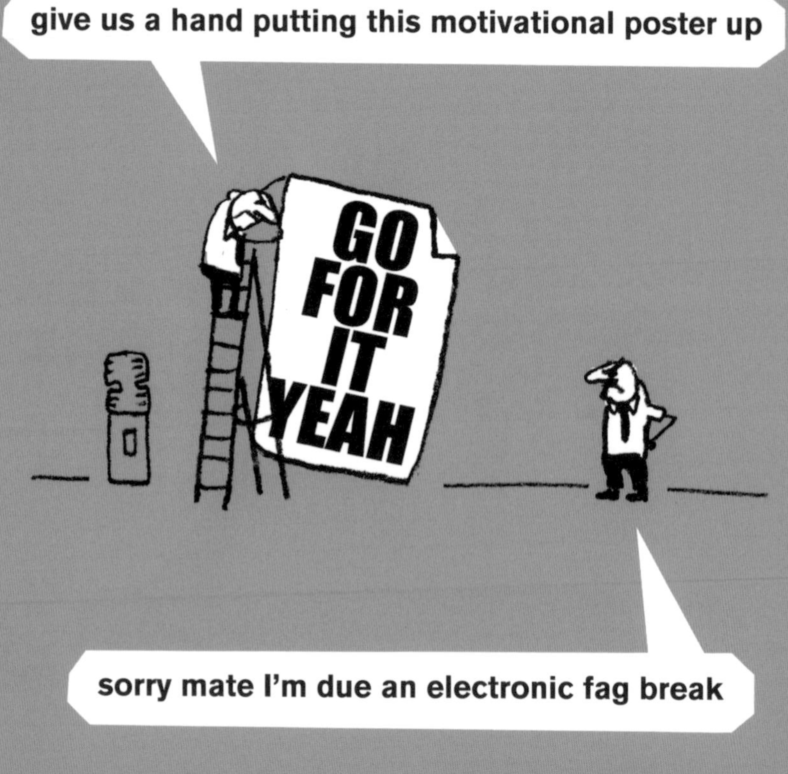
give us a hand putting this motivational poster up
GO FOR IT YEAH
sorry mate I'm due an electronic fag break

work

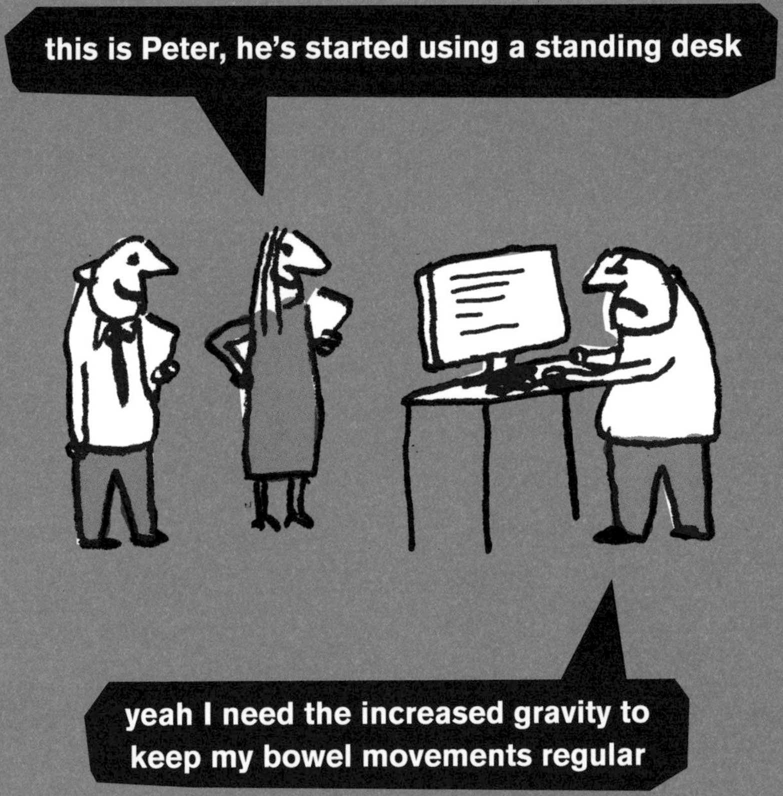
this is Peter, he’s started using a standing desk
yeah I need the increased gravity to keep my bowel movements regular

work

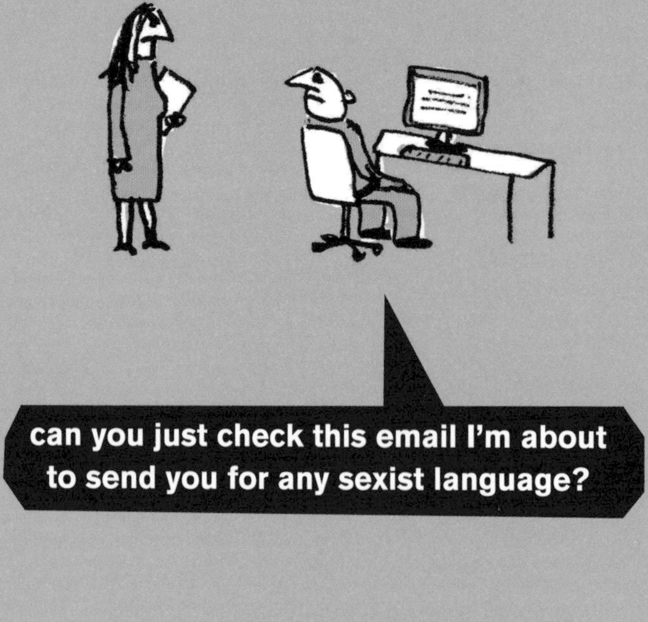
can you just check this email I'm about to send you for any sexist language?

work

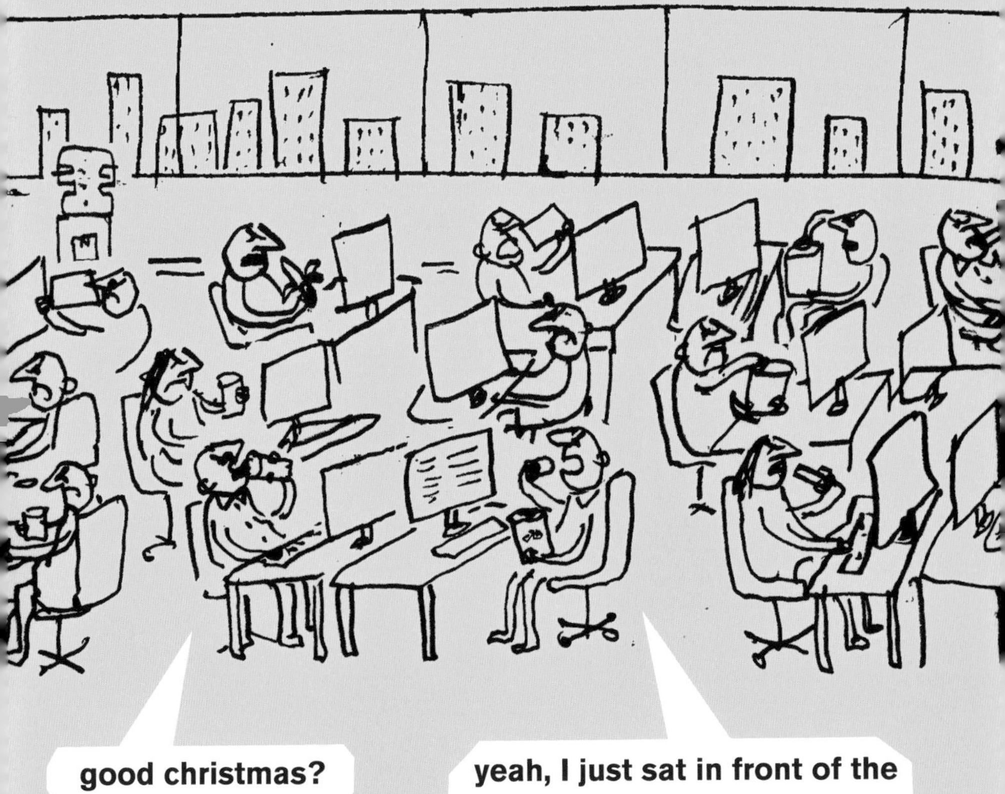
good christmas?
yeah, I just sat in front of the telly eating crisps all day

work

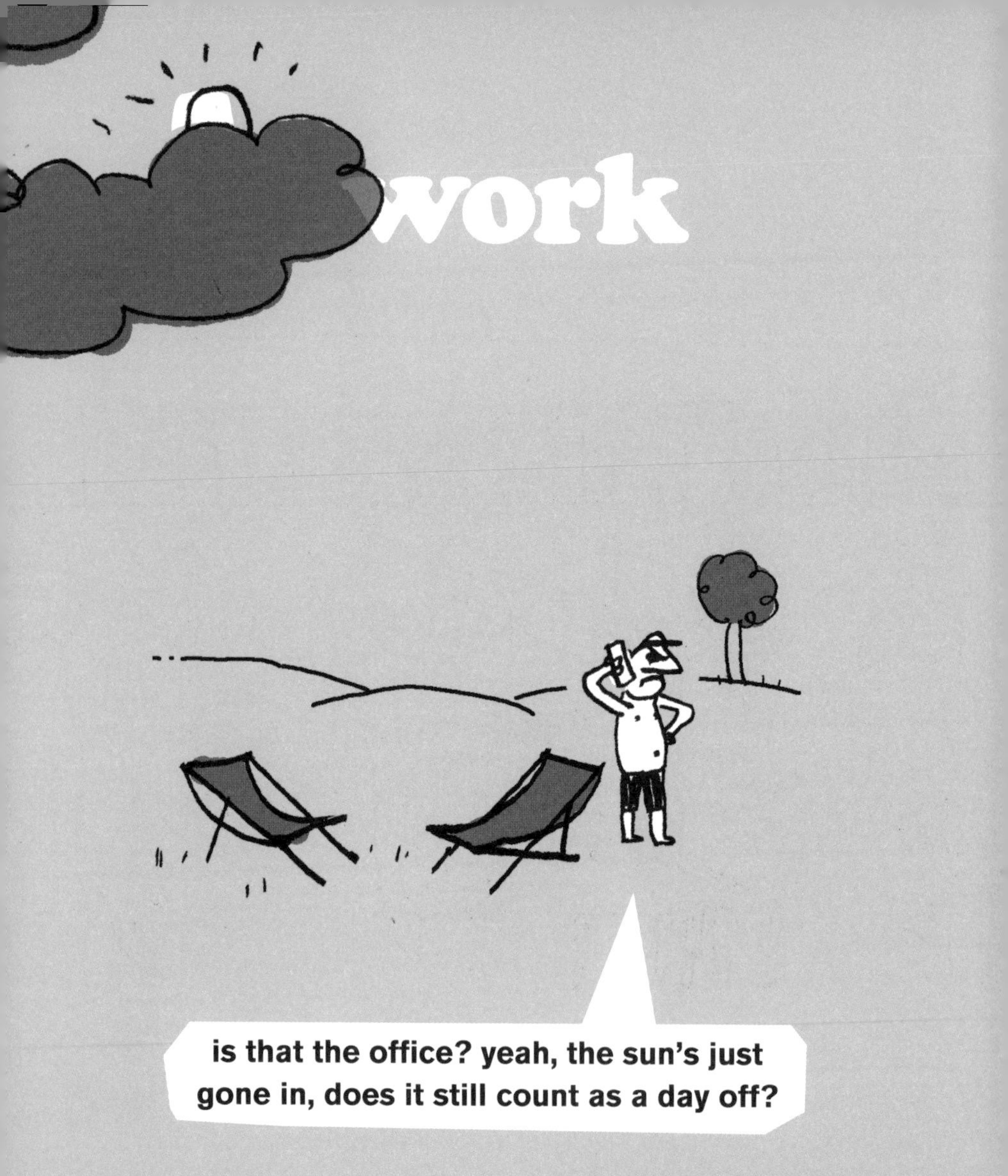
is that the office? yeah, the sun's just gone in, does it still count as a day off?

work

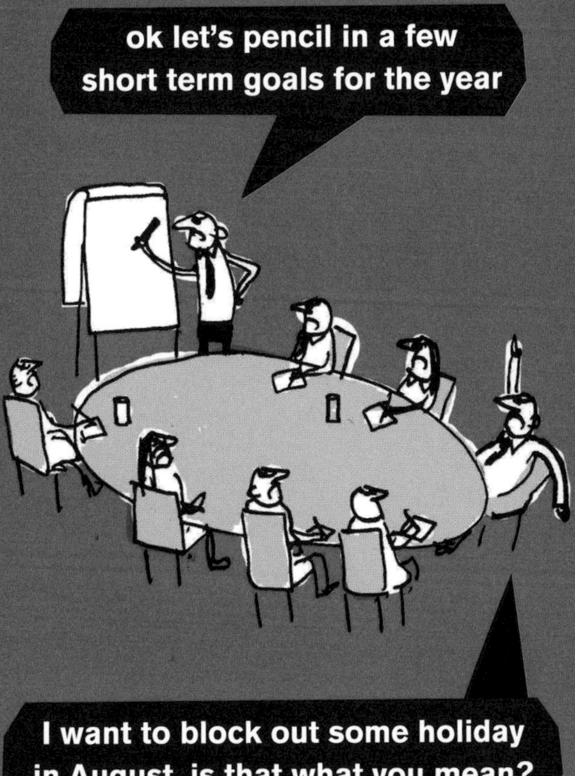
ok let's pencil in a few short term goals for the year
I want to block out some holiday in August, is that what you mean?

interview

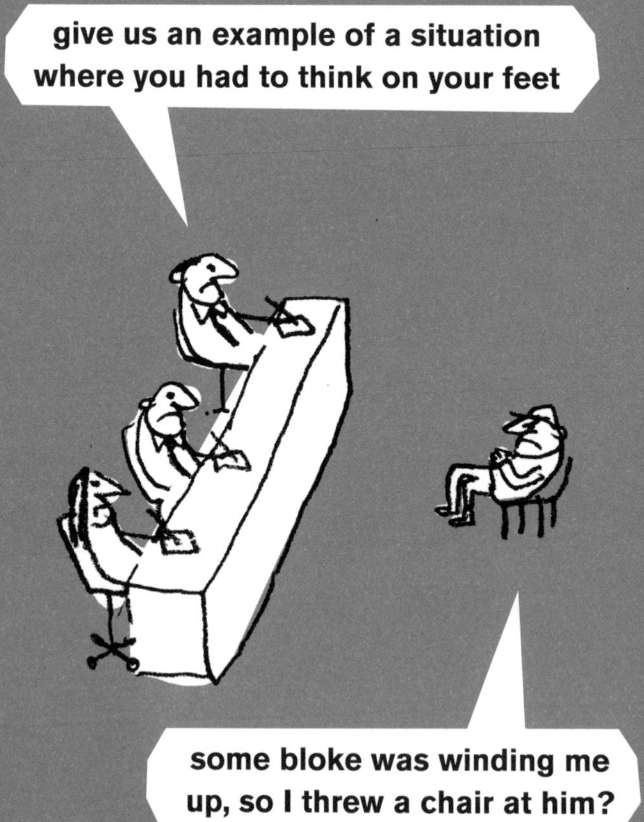
give us an example of a situation where you had to think on your feet
some bloke was winding me up, so I threw a chair at him?

work

I've been really enjoying working here since I started pretending it was some ropey reality TV show

work

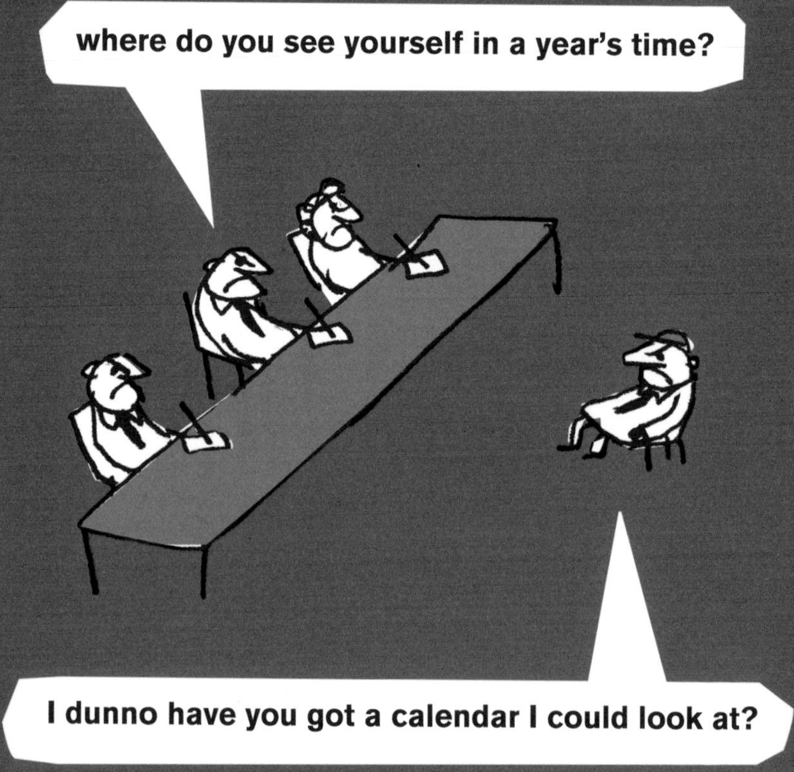
where do you see yourself in a year's time?
I dunno have you got a calendar I could look at?

work

I'm going home, I reckon I've got mild jet lag from them putting the clocks back

work

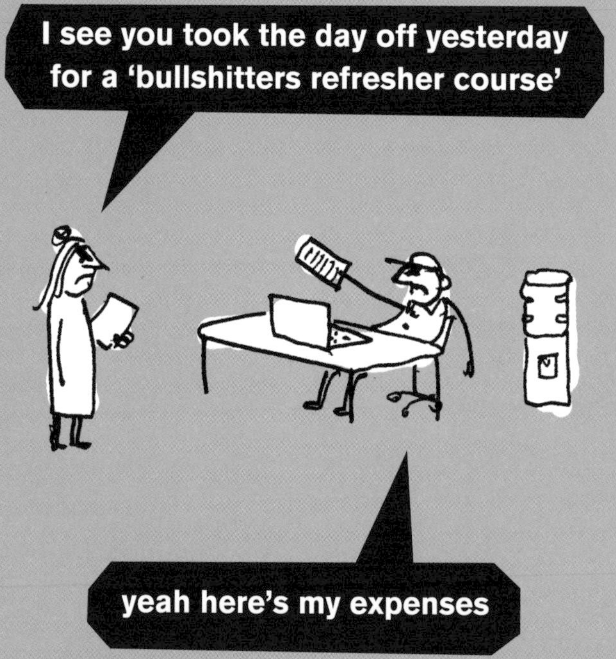
I see you took the day off yesterday for a 'bullshitters refresher course'
yeah here's my expenses

work

how would you feel about doing some courses to expand your skill set?
ok, but if I learn something useful I'll probably be off yeah

team player

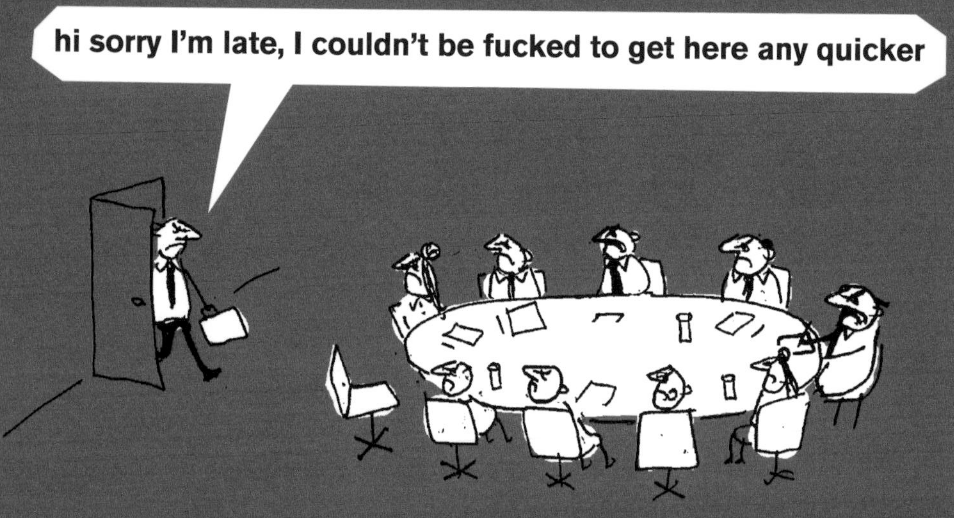
hi sorry I'm late, I couldn't be fucked to get here any quicker

work

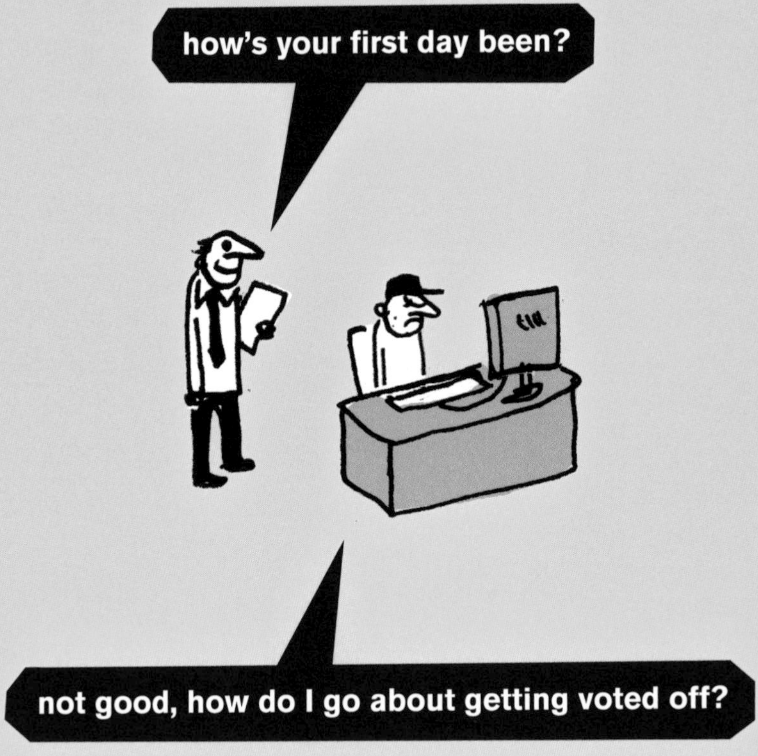
how's your first day been?
not good, how do I go about getting voted off?